Francis Frith's

Maidenhead
and the River Thames

Photographic Memories

Francis Frith's
Maidenhead
and the River Thames

Martin Andrew

FRITH
BOOK Co

First published in the United Kingdom in 2001 by
Frith Book Company Ltd

Paperback Edition 2001
ISBN 1-85937-339-9

British Library Cataloguing in Publication Data

Francis Frith's Maidenhead and the River Thames
Martin Andrew

Frith Book Company Ltd
Frith's Barn, Teffont,
Salisbury, Wiltshire SP3 5QP
Tel: +44 (0) 1722 716 376
Email: info@francisfrith.co.uk
www.francisfrith.co.uk

Printed and bound in Great Britain

Front Cover: Maidenhead, High Street 1911 63798

AS WITH ANY HISTORICAL DATABASE THE FRITH ARCHIVE IS CONSTANTLY BEING CORRECTED AND IMPROVED
AND THE PUBLISHERS WOULD WELCOME INFORMATION ON OMISSIONS OR INACCURACIES

Contents

Francis Frith: *Victorian Pioneer*

FRANCIS FRITH, Victorian founder of the world-famous photographic archive, was a complex and multi-talented man. A devout Quaker and a highly successful Victorian businessman, he was both philosophic by nature and pioneering in outlook.

By 1855 Francis Frith had already established a wholesale grocery business in Liverpool, and sold it for the astonishing sum of £200,000, which is the equivalent today of over £15,000,000. Now a multi-millionaire, he was able to indulge his passion for travel. As a child he had pored over travel books written by early explorers, and his fancy and imagination had been stirred by family holidays to the sublime mountain regions of Wales and Scotland. 'What a land of spirit-stirring and enriching scenes and places!' he had written. He was to return to these scenes of grandeur in later years to 'recapture the thousands of vivid and tender memories', but with a different purpose. Now in his thirties, and captivated by the new science of photography, Frith set out on a series of pioneering journeys to the Nile regions that occupied him from 1856 until 1860.

Intrigue and Adventure

He took with him on his travels a specially-designed wicker carriage that acted as both dark-room and sleeping chamber. These far-flung journeys were packed with intrigue and adventure. In his life story, written when he was sixty-three, Frith tells of being held captive by bandits, and of fighting 'an awful midnight battle to the very point of surrender with a deadly pack of hungry, wild dogs'. Sporting flowing Arab costume, Frith arrived at Akaba by camel seventy years before Lawrence, where he encountered 'desert princes and rival sheikhs, blazing with jewel-hilted swords'.

During these extraordinary adventures he was assiduously exploring the desert regions bordering the Nile and patiently recording the antiquities and peoples with his camera. He was the first photographer to venture beyond the sixth cataract. Africa was still the mysterious 'Dark Continent', and Stanley and Livingstone's historic meeting was a decade into the future. The conditions for picture taking confound belief. He laboured for hours in his wicker dark-room in the sweltering heat of the desert, while the volatile chemicals fizzed dangerously in their trays. Often he was forced to work in remote tombs and caves where conditions were cooler. Back in London he exhibited his photographs and was 'rapturously cheered' by members of the Royal Society. His reputation as a

photographer was made overnight. An eminent modern historian has likened their impact on the population of the time to that on our own generation of the first photographs taken on the surface of the moon.

Venture of a Life-Time

Characteristically, Frith quickly spotted the opportunity to create a new business as a specialist publisher of photographs. He lived in an era of immense and sometimes violent change. For the poor in the early part of Victoria's reign work was a drudge and the hours long, and people had precious little free time to enjoy themselves. Most had no transport other than a cart or gig at their disposal, and had not travelled far beyond the boundaries of their own town or village. However,

by the 1870s, the railways had threaded their way across the country, and Bank Holidays and half-day Saturdays had been made obligatory by Act of Parliament. All of a sudden the ordinary working man and his family were able to enjoy days out and see a little more of the world.

With characteristic business acumen, Francis Frith foresaw that these new tourists would enjoy having souvenirs to commemorate their days out. In 1860 he married Mary Ann Rosling and set out with the intention of photographing every city, town and village in Britain. For the next thirty years he travelled the country by train and by pony and trap, producing fine photographs of seaside resorts and beauty spots that were keenly bought by millions of Victorians. These prints were painstakingly pasted into family albums and pored over during the dark nights of winter, rekindling precious memories of summer excursions.

The Rise of Frith & Co

Frith's studio was soon supplying retail shops all over the country. To meet the demand he gathered about him a small team of photographers, and published the work of independent artist-photographers of the calibre of Roger Fenton and Francis Bedford. In order to gain some understanding of the scale of Frith's business one only has to look at the catalogue issued by Frith & Co in 1886: it runs to some 670 pages, listing not only many thousands of views of the British Isles but also many photographs of most European countries, and China, Japan, the USA and Canada — note the sample page shown above from the hand-written *Frith & Co* ledgers detailing pictures taken. By 1890 Frith had created the greatest specialist photographic publishing company in the world,

Frith's death, a new card measuring 5.5 x 3.5 inches became the standard format, but it was not until 1902 that the divided back came into being, with address and message on one face and a full-size illustration on the other. *Frith & Co* were in the vanguard of postcard development, and Frith's sons Eustace and Cyril continued their father's monumental task, expanding the number of views offered to the public and recording more and more places in Britain, as the coasts and countryside were opened up to mass travel.

Francis Frith died in 1898 at his villa in Cannes, his great project still growing. The archive he created continued in business for another seventy years. By 1970 it contained over a third of a million pictures of 7,000 cities, towns and villages. The massive photographic record Frith has left to us stands as a living monument to a special and very remarkable man.

with over 2,000 outlets – more than the combined number that Boots and WH Smith have today! The picture on the right shows the *Frith & Co* display board at Ingleton in the Yorkshire Dales. Beautifully constructed with mahogany frame and gilt inserts, it could display up to a dozen local scenes.

Postcard Bonanza

The ever-popular holiday postcard we know today took many years to develop. In 1870 the Post Office issued the first plain cards, with a pre-printed stamp on one face. In 1894 they allowed other publishers' cards to be sent through the mail with an attached adhesive halfpenny stamp. Demand grew rapidly, and in 1895 a new size of postcard was permitted called the court card, but there was little room for illustration. In 1899, a year after

Frith's Archive: *A Unique Legacy*

FRANCIS FRITH'S legacy to us today is of immense significance and value, for the magnificent archive of evocative photographs he created provides a unique record of change in 7,000 cities, towns and villages throughout Britain over a century and more. Frith and his fellow studio photographers revisited locations many times down the years to update their views, compiling for us an enthralling and colourful pageant of British life and character.

We tend to think of Frith's sepia views of Britain as nostalgic, for most of us use them to conjure up memories of places in our own lives with which we have family associations. It often makes us forget that to Francis Frith they were records of daily life as it was actually being lived in the cities, towns and villages of his day. The Victorian age was one of great and often bewildering change for ordinary people, and though the pictures evoke an impression of slower times, life was as busy and hectic as it is today.

We are fortunate that Frith was a photographer of the people, dedicated to recording the minutiae of everyday life. For it is this sheer wealth of visual data, the painstaking chronicle of changes in dress, transport, street layouts, buildings, housing, engineering and landscape that captivates us so much today. His remarkable images offer us a powerful link with the past and with the lives of our ancestors.

Today's Technology

Computers have now made it possible for Frith's many thousands of images to be accessed almost instantly. In the Frith archive today, each photograph is carefully 'digitised' then stored on a CD Rom. Frith archivists can locate a single photograph amongst thousands within seconds. Views can be catalogued and sorted under a variety of categories of place and content to the immediate benefit of researchers.

Inexpensive reference prints can be created for them at the touch of a mouse button, and a wide range of books and other printed materials assembled and published for a wider, more general readership - in the next twelve months over a hundred Frith local history titles will be published! The day-to-day workings of the archive are very different from how they were in Francis Frith's time: imagine the herculean task of sorting through eleven tons of glass negatives as Frith had to do to locate a particular sequence of pictures! Yet

THE FRANCIS FRITH COLLECTION
Photographic publishers since 1860

HOME | PHOTO SEARCH | BOOKS | PORTFOLIO | GALLERY | MY CART
Products | History | Other Collections | Contact us | Help?

your town,
your village

365,000 photographs of 7,000 towns and villages, taken between 1860 & 1970.

The Frith Archive
The Frith Archive is the remarkable legacy of its energetic and visionary founder. Today, the Frith archive is the only nationally important archive of its kind still in private ownership.

The Collection is world-renowned for the extraordinary quality of its images.

The Gallery
This month The Frith Gallery features images from "Frith's Egypt".

News...
Image update complete.
An additional 5,000 images have been added and the quality of all images has now been improved.

Sample Chapters avaliable.
The first selection of sample chapters from the Frith Book Co.'s extensive range is now available. All are offered in Pdf format for easy downloading and viewing.

explore
FRITH
Search thousands of photographs from one of the worlds' great archives.

Town search

County search
Select a county

the FRITHgallery

See Frith at www.francisfrith.co.uk

the archive still prides itself on maintaining the same high standards of excellence laid down by Francis Frith, including the painstaking cataloguing and indexing of every view.

It is curious to reflect on how the internet now allows researchers in America and elsewhere greater instant access to the archive than Frith himself ever enjoyed. Many thousands of individual views can be called up on screen within seconds on one of the Frith internet sites, enabling people living continents away to revisit the streets of their ancestral home town, or view places in Britain where they have enjoyed holidays. Many overseas researchers welcome the chance to view special theme selections, such as transport, sports, costume and ancient monuments.

We are certain that Francis Frith would have heartily approved of these modern developments in imaging techniques, for he himself was always working at the very limits of Victorian photographic technology.

The Value of the Archive Today

Because of the benefits brought by the computer, Frith's images are increasingly studied by social historians, by researchers into genealogy and ancestory, by architects, town planners, and by teachers and schoolchildren involved in local history projects.

In addition, the archive offers every one of us an opportunity to examine the places where we and our families have lived and worked down the years. Highly successful in Frith's own era, the archive is now, a century and more on, entering a new phase of popularity.

The Past in Tune with the Future

Historians consider the Francis Frith Collection to be of prime national importance. It is the only archive of its kind remaining in private ownership and has been valued at a million pounds. However, this figure is now rapidly increasing as digital technology enables more and more people around the world to enjoy its benefits.

Francis Frith's archive is now housed in an historic timber barn in the beautiful village of Teffont in Wiltshire. Its founder would not recognize the archive office as it is today. In place of the many thousands of dusty boxes containing glass plate negatives and an all-pervading odour of photographic chemicals, there are now ranks of computer screens. He would be amazed to watch his images travelling round the world at unimaginable speeds through network and internet lines.

The archive's future is both bright and exciting. Francis Frith, with his unshakeable belief in making photographs available to the greatest number of people, would undoubtedly approve of what is being done today with his lifetime's work. His photographs, depicting our shared past, are now bringing pleasure and enlightenment to millions around the world a century and more after his death.

Maidenhead - *An Introduction*

LIKE READING AND High Wycombe, its near neighbours west of London, Maidenhead in Berkshire suffered greatly in the 1960s when much of its historic fabric was wantonly destroyed. This was in the era when the common belief was that a town could only be hauled from its economic doldrums through rebuilding as much as possible in the latest style. This was a tragedy, as 1960s commercial architecture was almost universally appalling - indeed, many of those buildings are now being demolished and replaced by better ones, both in design and constructional quality terms.

However, while Reading's centre was big enough to absorb a lot of damage and High Wycombe's fine medieval parish church, Georgian Guildhall and Little Market House ensured continued coherence and character, the problem for Maidenhead was

that it had appreciably less to lose, making the depredation of the historic core appear far worse.

During the 1960s, the Victorian Town hall and the reworked Georgian/Victorian parish church were knocked down and replaced with modern buildings. Fortunately, Smyth's Almshouses of 1659 survived, but these are east of the town centre and contribute nothing to the townscape. Indeed most of Bridge Street between the Almshouses and Chapel Arches, most of King Street and much of Broadway and lower Queen Street have been entirely rebuilt, while the inner relief road/by-pass, comprising Frascati, Bad-Godesberg Way and St Cloud Way, cut a swathe close to the town centre as they sweep north and west. Castle Hill is cut off by a large roundabout from the High Street and the splendid Clock Tower now resides in a dual

carriageway island near the railway station.

That said, there have been attempts to make amends: the west end of the High Street is now pedestrianised, as is the upper part of King Street, and interpretation plaques tell visitors about important buildings and events. Kidwells Park survives, albeit cut off by Bad-Goseberg Way, as does the Technical Institute and School of Art on Marlow Road where Stanley Spencer studied. It is now a social services centre run by the guardians of Maidenhead's surviving historic core, the Royal Borough of Windsor and Maidenhead.

This book is very much an historic record of central Maidenhead as it was in the past - so much has now gone. Sufficient remnants do exist, however, for us to piece the story together, recognise surviving buildings, and trace their story. Outside Maidenhead the story is very different. The town grew up on higher ground inland of the flood-prone River Thames, but its river crossing is the key to Maidenhead's growth and development. In the second half of the 19th century the river changed from a trade artery to one increasingly orientated towards leisure, and the town cashed in on this great boating boom. Development along the river itself and in the area between it and the town flourished: by the late 19th century the riverside was thriving with hotels, boathouses where you could hire anything from a large steam launch to a humble punt, and the houses of the well-to-do and the middle classes. By the 1880s, Boulters Lock,

built in 1772 to by-pass Ray Mill and its weir, had over a thousand pleasure craft of all descriptions passing through on a Summer Sunday.

This area has also seen recent changes with quite a few of the large houses, including the old Ray Mead Hotel, being replaced by blocks of flats, but it still retains its leafy suburban character. Later, we'll take an imaginary cruise downstream from Medmenham to Dorney, with the odd landward excursions to places like Holyport and Cookham Dean, but in this Introduction we focus on Maidenhead and its two superb bridges over the River Thames.

Originally, and certainly by the 11th century, Maidenhead was based on North Town, but the presence of the King's Highway from London to Bath led to rapid settlement in an east-west alignment along the main road, which crossed the Thames by ferry half a mile to the east. The town grew up on either side of the stream known nowadays as the York Stream, but formerly called the Dunmede Dyche. It had been a navigable channel branching from the Thames near Cookham to re-enter the main river in what is now the Fishery Estate south of the railway bridge, but it silted up during the 17th century.

Once part of Cookham and Bray parishes, Maidenhead had emerged into independence by the 13th century. Its trade was based on the tolls collected from through traffic using the new bridge that had replaced the ferry around 1280. The new

bridge had been a timber one, not the present fine stone bridge, which is a replacement from the 1770s.

By the mid-18th century, Maidenhead was much the same size as in medieval and Tudor times: a single main street ran east-west from the Smyth's Almshouses to the foot of Castle Hill, then called Folly Hill. The street was lined with coaching inns such as the Sun, the Bear and the White Hart, other inns including the Swan, and shops and houses.

The town had a small Guildhall, demolished when the Victorian town hall was built, and the parish church of St Mary's, which dated from at least the mid-15th-century. These two buildings occupied the centre of the High Street's eastern end. It appears that a chapel of St Andrew and St Mary Magdalene was sited on or near Chapel Arches, the bridge over the York Stream. This was a chapel of ease, founded about 1270; it may have become the first parish church when Maidenhead evolved into a separate parish. Sources seem unclear as to whether there were two churches or not, but there is no longer a sign of one church - never mind two - in this main street location.

Maidenhead gained a mayor and a borough corporation by Royal Charter in 1582, but remained a small town, continuing as a place of rest and preparation for the coaching trade prior to the haul up Castle Hill onto Maidenhead Thicket. Until the early 19th century, this area was a haunt of the highwaymen who held up the stage coaches and carriages to rob their traveller occupants; apparently the famous Dick Turpin can be counted amongst these.

In 1826 Maidenhead had a mere 192 houses and 945 inhabitants. Its medieval church had been rebuilt in 1724 and was still in the middle of the High Street; in 1824 it was moved by an Act of Parliament to clear the highway of a notorious obstruction. The Georgian brick box was re-erected, but in the process turned into a Gothic one more acceptable to 1820s' tastes. This church, seen in a few views in the book, was condemned by the church architect in the 1960s and replaced by a modern effort in 1964.

However, great changes crept up on Maidenhead in the 1830s. In June 1838, Isambard Kingdom Brunel's Great Western Railway, having reached the Buckinghamshire side of the River Thames en route from Paddington, opened Maidenhead Riverside Station at Taplow. In 1839, the railway crossed the river, and by 1841 it had reached Bristol. This (of course) virtually destroyed the coaching trade overnight, drastically reducing the toll income from the road bridge and forcing Maidenhead to adapt rapidly. Worst of all, there was no station on the Maidenhead side of the river to attract traffic directly into the town centre.

The road bridge had been rebuilt between 1772 and 1777, using the noted architect Sir Robert Taylor as its designer and costing £19,000. Its seven rusticated arches and elegant balustraded parapet

symbolised the town and county's pride and the wealth generated by the coach trade, which was then at its peak. Sixty years later, the railway arrived with a bridge demonstrating a breathtaking architectural audacity that befitted the brash newcomer. Restricted to two arches by the local powers-that-be, Brunel crossed the river with two immense, almost flat brick-arched spans, each 128 feet across, which critics said could not possibly survive a day, let alone 150 years. Widened in the 1890s, it still carries hundreds of fast and heavy trains every day with aplomb, and will no doubt continue to do so for many more years.

Maidenhead achieved a station of sorts in 1854, when the Wycombe Railway opened a branch line to High Wycombe via Cookham and Bourne End. Boyne Hill Station, halfway up Castle Hill, served this purpose until the present Maidenhead Station opened in 1871, after which Boyne Hill was closed. By this time the town had woken up and a number of prominent tradesmen, lawyers, bankers, brewers and other citizens dragged the town out of the mail coach era and into the railway age. By 1866 the population had expanded to about 5,000, but by the 1911 Census it had trebled to 15,218. By now a Victorian town had emerged with a new street lay-out, involving a great deal of rebuilding and town planning.

As the innkeepers lost business, a new wave of entrepreneurs emerged to replace them, many local, others from elsewhere. Like many a Victorian

group of the day, the town's shopkeepers, brewers, professionals and traders showed drive, determination, ambition and enterprise. They prospered, bought and developed land around the town and, having formerly lived above their shops and offices, moved into smart new villas on Castle Hill or in Norfolk Park. The leading lights in this expansion formed the Maidenhead Improvement Company and the town grew mightily, with many of these enterprising men becoming mayor in due course.

In 1872, Queen Street was laid out and over the next thirty years the area between the 1871 railway station and the town was developed commercially. A town hall was built in the fashionable Italianate style seen in Kensington and Ladbroke Grove. The developers did not neglect the spiritual needs of the new citizens: All Saints, Boyne Hill, St Luke's, St Mark and other churches were built; there were also several nonconformist churches and chapels built, including the Methodist Church of 1859 and St Joseph's Roman Catholic Church of 1884. Temporal needs were also met with schools being built, including All Saints School of 1857 and the County School of 1894. In 1895 the town acquired a Technical Institute and Drill Hall, both on Marlow Road, while Kidwell Park was given to the town by Mayor Pearce in 1890.

The road bridge tolls were finally abolished in 1903. The town expanded to the north, west and south, the railway station providing fast connections

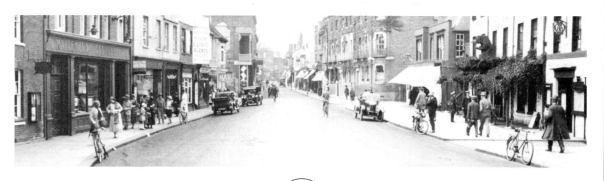

to London and other towns. The middle classes produced by Maidenhead's Victorian growth were more than supplemented by a new group: commuters.

East of the town, development was slower, which was unsurprising given that the area between the York Stream and the River Thames was notoriously prone to disastrous flooding. Also, much of the land was occupied by the grounds of Ray Lodge on the north side of Bridge Road and Oldfield Lodge on the south. However, the river leisure boom changed all that, and the whole area was developed over a longer period, starting in the 1870s and peaking around 1900, despite the disastrous floods of 1894.

It is said that many of the houses along the river north of Maidenhead Bridge were built by rich guards officers for their mistresses, the latter being banned from sleeping in the Brigade of Guards Boat Club premises on the Buckinghamshire bank. Whether this was the case or not, a number of prestigious hotels were built which ensured Maidenhead's social success as a riverside resort town, complete with a Promenade along the river bank. The Thames Hotel, Skindles, Ray Mead and the Riviera could accommodate large numbers of fashionable visitors, while the new housing on the former Ray Lodge estate was aimed at the well-heeled middle classes.

The late 19th century saw a quite spectacular growth in leisure pursuits, and this enthusiasm percolated down to the working classes. The great boating boom was a concrete demonstration of increased Victorian and Edwardian affluence and leisure, mostly focused on Saturday afternoons and Sundays. Maidenhead was quick to exploit this Golden Age. The boom was wonderfully evoked in Jerome K Jerome's 1889 classic 'Three Men in a Boat', although the author portrayed Maidenhead as too upmarket for his lower-middle class clerks. However, the truth was that at Maidenhead office clerks and their girls could rub shoulders with haughty mi'lords in the bustle of Boulters Lock on any Summer Sunday. Boating continues to be as popular today, and Maidenhead's river frontage and Boulters Lock are still bustling places.

In the town, however, there was decline after World War II. The Council attempted to address this with its 1961 town development plan, which proposed the current by-pass, shopping centres and multi-storey car parks amongst other things. A lot was pulled down, including the Victorian Town Hall and part of Queen Street, to make way for the 'brave new world' office tower of Berkshire House, designed by Hildebrand and Glicker - a 12-storey slap in the face for the old coaching town. The presence of Kidwells Park gave the by-pass an easy passage through its southern part. A municipal campus emerged on St Ives Road, the wan Neo-Georgian Town Hall of 1962 occupied the west side of the road, while the old Free Library, a distinguished building of 1904, was replaced in 1973 by the present stylish modern one.

Looking at the 1960s buildings, including the awful 54-70 North Bridge Road (which stands empty in 2001) and Berkshire House, one cannot help wishing that the plan had been drawn up 20 years later, when the value of older buildings was more appreciated. However, it was not to be, and many roads are now lined with and overwhelmed by characterless modern office blocks. Certainly, the Victorian businessman alighting from his train at Maidenhead today would recognise little more than the Clock Tower from the town he knew (and that only arrived in 1899), for screening his view of the old town centre are many 1980s and 1990s office blocks.

That having been said, there is still a vibrancy about in the town. The Nicholson Centre, the shopping centre south of the High Street that occupies the site of the Victoria Nicholson's brewery and much besides, is a great success. Sufficient of the old town (as seen in this collection of photographs) remains as a tribute to the dynamism that transformed the old coaching town into a major commercial centre in a remarkably short time; along the river, the two great bridges and much of the riverside architecture survives. On a less cheery note, Bond's rotting boatyard buildings will not be around much longer and Skindles remains boarded up. Traffic remains a problem, but once you have parked and become a pedestrian, the town and river front reward you richly.

Maidenhead Town Centre

Maidenhead
Bridge Street 1911 63803
The A4 now by-passes the town to the north, while the old Bath
Road continues through its heart. This section of Bridge Street is
now called New Bridge Road. Only the Moor Tavern on the right
and the stucco house beyond now survive, as offices. The parapet
in the foreground belongs to the Moor Arches bridge. This was
severely damaged in the 1894 floods and then repaired, before
being replaced by the present concrete balustraded bridge.

Maidenhead, Bridge Street 1890 23633
Further in towards town, Bridge Street, now called Moor Bridge Road, has seen dramatic changes. The still-surviving Carpenters Arms on the right is now Club La Costa. Beyond, the modern Forelease Road now cuts through. The buildings on the left have made way for a Waitrose supermarket. In the distance is Chapel Arches Bridge and the tower of the old parish church.

Maidenhead, Bridge Street c1955 M7016
We are looking eastwards away from the town centre, past the Crown Lane/Bridge Avenue junction. The 1930s Crown Hotel is now the Newt and Cucumber. The building beyond, built as a model lodging house, is now the Royal British Legion. Three doors along from the Legion, a 17th-century building survives in heavily restored form as Jonathan's Pizza and Pasta. The single storey building on the right has been stylishly rebuilt as a Pizza Express.

▼ **Maidenhead, Bridge Street c1955** M7015
We have moved further west to the junction with St Ives Road,
looking east. The Bear Hotel on the left has an early 19th-century
stucco front; further on are the Chapel Arches. The building on the
left with the urns along its parapet (which do not survive) is part of
High Street Colonnade, a 1930 development in Adam style built along
the north side of the Chapel Arches bridge.

▼ **Maidenhead, High Street 1890** 23654
From the start of Chapel Arches bridge, we are looking west along the High Street
from Bridge Street. The Bear Hotel is on the right and the stucco house beyond
survives, now Michael Chell's Menswear. The elegant mid-19th-century terrace
beyond survives as a façade to 1980s offices, with an added mansard storey.

▲ **Maidenhead
Bear Hotel 1890** 23635
The original Bear Hotel
was further up the High
Street, near the present
junction with Queen
Street. The present hotel,
with its pediment and the
bear mascot's eyes
glowing red, is early
19th-century. The
building on the right, J B
Tyler wine merchant, is
now part of the Bear. To
the left can be seen the
tower of the now rebuilt
parish church.

◄ **Maidenhead High Street, looking West 1903** 50834

This view is from Chapel Arches bridge. Rebuilt in 1825, its name comes from its medieval predecessor, which had the Chapel of Saints Andrew and Mary Magdalene nearby. The chapel was founded about 1270 and may have been either the forerunner of the parish church or a separate chapel.

▼ **Maidenhead, High Street 1911** 63799

A car is a blur compared with the cycle and horses it is overtaking. The building on the far left, built in 1909 for the Maidenhead Gas Company, replaced the one in the 1890 view (see 23634, page 20). The view of the Bear and the adjacent buildings on the right is now hidden by High Street Colonnade. Built on the east side of the bridge in 1930, this was a Neo-Adam confection of shops with flats above.

▼ **Maidenhead, High Street 1921** 70909

Again cars dominate the 1921 scene, this being the main A4 London to Bath road until the by-pass was built in the 1960s. The west-bound traffic, overtaking a parked vehicle and cyclist, is rather hogging the middle of the road. The area in front of the Bear Hotel has now been extended into the road to provide space for outside tables.

▲ **Maidenhead High Street and Town Hall 1903** 50833

The Victorian Town Hall and the tobacconist beyond were shamefully demolished in 1962 and replaced by the appalling Berkshire House, a three-storey block with a further nine-storey office tower above. The tobacconist stood at the corner of Queen Street and one assumes the building of Berkshire House financed the new Town Hall in St Ives Road - but at what cost to Maidenhead's townscape?

◄ **Maidenhead High Street 1911** 63797
The 1880s bank on the other side of the Queen Street junction survives today as Lloyds TSB. Beyond is R Martin, the drapers and ladieswear shop, a confident building dated 1903. Wyatt, the tailor and hatter on the right, survives as an altered building. So does the baker advertising Daren Bread, although the oriel bay window to its first floor tea-room has since gone.

**Maidenhead
High Street 1911**
63798
Here we are Looking east past the junction of Queen Street. W & R Fletcher, the tobacconists, occupies the corner spot. The building in front of the cluster of chimneys is A Upson, the chemist. It went in 1922 to be replaced by the Midland Bank, now HSBC, while the Town Hall to its right and Fletchers survived into the 1960s.

◄ **Maidenhead
High Street 1925** 70908
West of the Queen Street
junction the London-Bath A4
was remarkably narrow, but
now pedestrianised and by-
passed. This view looks east
Many buildings survive, apar
from the 1890s mock-Tudor
Barclays Bank, which was
rebuilt in the 1980s. The
pediments to its left were
'modernised' in the 1960s v
a straight parapet, while on
right there is now an entran
to the Nicholson Centre, a
modern shopping precinct c
the site of Nicholson's
Pineapple Brewery.

◄ **Maidenhead
High Street 1925**

77633

Moving back east for this 1925 view, Martin's the Drapers with its corner turret can be seen in the distance on the far left. Until 1824 the parish church of St Mary occupied much of the middle of the road and was the cause of much traffic difficulty for the stage coaches, carriers carts and other road users.

▼ **Maidenhead
High Street c1955** M7014

Back at the Queen Street junction, W & R Fletcher still has a few years to survive. The Midland Bank, now HSBC, replaced Upson's the chemists in 1922 with a single-storey building in typical 'Bankers' Baroque' style. The buildings beyond and many on the left past the Market Street junction have gone. The Queen Street corner is now occupied by the monstrous Berkshire House office block.

◄ **Maidenhead
High Street c1965** M7082

Further west, towards the King Street junction, this view records the curiously disjointed nature of this end of the High Street. The old Macfisheries building on the right, dated 1888, towers over a cottage-scale building with dormers. On the left is the grand Jacobean post office - its foundation stone was laid by Mayor Simpson in 1892 and it was completed in 1894. In the distance is the nearly new tower of the Berkshire House office block.

**Maidenhead
Queen Street 1904**
52373
Queen Street, originally
named New Road, was
laid out in 1872 by the
Maidenhead
Improvement Company,
a consortium of local
landowners and
businessmen. Here we
look south from High
Street. The left hand
side, the first and most
co-ordinated phase, has
a distinctive urban
quality with its row of
fashionable Italianate
façades. The first two
buildings went for the
1960s Berkshire House
development, but some
of the street's quality
still survives.

◀ **Maidenhead
King Street 1904** 52372
This is a much-changed
scene along the road leading
to Maidenhead Station, for
virtually nothing now
survives of King Street's
earlier buildings. Broadway
still exists, but now much
wider and with a multi-storey
car park on the right, while
Tesco's and the Nicholson
Centre shopping mall take
up most of the rest on the
right. The Rose pub (1881)
in the distance and the
Methodist Church (1859) are
all that remain on the left.

◀ Maidenhead
Queen Street 1911 63804

Further development southwards was held up and the architectural variety shows this. The terrace at the left survives but on the right all beyond the 1880s bank (now Atkinson and Keene estate agents) has been demolished, as far along as the parapeted building. The tall, hipped roof building had been the popular Brock's Café. The pub in the right foreground, on the Broadway junction, was rebuilt in the 1950s and is now Finnegan's Wake.

▼ Maidenhead
Clock Tower 1903 50835

This view is taken from the railway bridge on Brunel's Great Western Railway line from Paddington to Bristol, opened in 1841. Maidenhead only secured a station in 1871 and this spurred the development of King Street. The station approach became a sort of square, finally embellished by the Clock Tower. Apart from the Clock Tower, virtually all this has been rebuilt, including Nicholson's Brewery, whose chimney is seen in this view.

◀ Maidenhead
King Street and Clock Tower 1911 63801

Back at ground level we see the buildings that grew up around the station in the 1880s and 1890s, including Horley and Sons, corn and coal merchants, Vevers and Sons, plumbers and decorators, and Carter's, who arranged funerals and hired carriages. Behind the Clock Tower is another coal and coke merchant, Jeayes and Kasner - such businesses always flourish near railway stations. The buildings in this view have been replaced by smart and large office blocks, along with a multi-screen cinema.

**Maidenhead
Castle Hill 1904** 52381
This view is from the far
west end of the High
Street; the road on the
left is the start of King
Street. The Methodist
Church on the left
survives, but beyond is
the massive roundabout
where the by-pass cuts
across the foot of Castle
hill. Walls now prevent
much of a view up
Castle hill from here.
Everything near the
camera has now gone.
In the distance is the
Ice House, which does
survive.

**Maidenhead
Castle Hill 1904** 52380
This view is from beside
the Ice House, its
balcony covered in
creeper, looking back
down Castle Hill. All on
the left beyond the
monkey puzzle tree (now
gone) has been
demolished and the left-
hand railings have been
renewed. On the right,
the house dated 1882
still stands at the corner
of East Road, part of the
High Town developments
of the 1870s onwards.

◄ **Maidenhead
Castle Hill, looking west
1904** 52378
The foreground is now
occupied by the by-pass
roundabout, so the buildings
on the right, including the Sun
Inn, have been demolished.
Houses and villas beyond
remain, including what are
now Spring Lodge and Kent
Lodge (formerly the Ice
House), the tall building
beyond the liveried coachman.
It was built over ice wells and
used by a Mr Hamblett, a local
fishmonger. Now a pair of
houses, it has lost its Waterloo
balconies.

▼ **Maidenhead
Castle Hill 1911** 63806
We are at the foot of Castle
Hill. Most of this area is now
the enormous by-pass
roundabout. The Edwardian
shops on the left have gone,
as well as much on the right
(the Ice House is again visible
in the distance). The portico
belongs to what had been
one of Maidenhead's main
coaching inns, the Sun Inn.
Later a doctor's house and
surgery, the name went to a
building next door, just uphill.

◄ **Maidenhead
Castle Hill, looking west
1904** 52377
19 Castle Hill is a late 19th-
century, mock-castle style
house, complete with
battlements. It was built in
London stock brick-kiln slag
with stone dressings. Indeed
Castle Hill was originally
named Folly Hill, but residents
felt Castle Hill had more tone.
The Wycombe Railway
Company burrowed through
the hill here and from 1854
until 1871 this was the only
Maidenhead station on the
town side of the river. It was
named Boyne Hill Station.

Churches and Other Buildings

Maidenhead
St Mary's Church 1903 50836
Having replaced the medieval parish church of 1724, this church was sited closer to Chapel Arches where it
constricted the Bath Road. An 1822 Act of Parliament secured its relocation north of the High Street. As it was
rebuilt, it was Gothicised, its pretty Georgian cupola being replaced by a heavy belfry stage. This was all for nothing;
it was demolished in 1962 and rebuilt with a glass fibre spire to designs by Lord Mottistone and Paul Paget.

Maidenhead, Town Hall c1960 M7072
The Victorian Town Hall reflected the new pride of the town's prosperous citizens, although the forecourt meant it was not seen in views along the High Street. It was also outflanked by the Queen Street development of 1872. However, it did close the vista down Market Street. Both it and the Minor House, formerly Fletcher's the tobacconist, made way in the early 1960s for Berkshire House; a new Town Hall was built on St Ives Road.

Maidenhead, Technical School and New Drill Hall 1903 50837
Along the Marlow Road at the west end of Kidwell's Park is the former Technical School, dated 1895. It was designed in Domestic Revival style by local architect E J Shrewsbury, who also designed the Clock Tower, St Paul's Church and many other local buildings. Beyond is the Drill Hall. Now demolished, its site is occupied by the Commonwealth War Graves Commission headquarters of 1974. Stanley Spencer, from nearby Cookham, studied art at the Technical Institute.

Maidenhead, Clock Tower 1911 63802
One of Maidenhead's best-known landmarks is the Clock Tower, near the station, at the south end of King Street.
Now on a traffic island and difficult to approach, it commemorated Queen Victoria's Diamond Jubilee in 1897.
Funded by public subscription, the foundation stone was laid on 7 November 1899 by the mayor, John Truscott,
and the architect was E J Shrewsbury. Behind, it all has gone to be replaced by a four-storey 1990s office block,
King's Chase.

Maidenhead, Free Library 1904 53148
A proud modern library, built in 1973, has replaced the old Free Library in St Ives Road, shown here while very new. Built and opened in 1904, it was funded by public subscription and donations. American philanthropist Andrew Carnegie, whose library donations can be found all over the country, was a significant donor, as was Alderman Nicholson.

Maidenhead, Free Library 1904 53149
Another view shows what a high quality design the subscribers got from their architects, Arthur McKewan and G H V Cole, using a sort of Baroque-cum-Wren style. It cost £6,000. The cedar survived from the grounds of Ives Place, a mansion and later an hotel, which stood where the present 1962 Town Hall is located.

Maidenhead, War Memorial 1921 70910
The memorial to Maidenhead's First World War dead was erected in 1921, north of the library. Frith's photographers in the 1920s particularly favoured war memorial views, for they were very popular as postcards so soon after the War's end. Names were added for World War II and the memorial is now on the other side of St Ives Road, in the forecourt of Sir Hubert Worthington and Guy North's 1962 Town Hall.

Maidenhead, Boyne Hill and All Saints Church 1911 63810
As Maidenhead expanded, largely guided by a number of local entrepreneurs, the provision of churches and similar facilities was a crucial element in their planning. The best of the churches was All Saints on Boyne Hill, seen here from Rutland Road. The different colour roof tiles show where Arthur Street has just added two further bays to the nave (in 1911) of his father George Edmund Street's 1854 church.

Maidenhead, All Saints Church 1911 63812
Arthur Street also linked what had been a detached bell tower, itself an 1865 addition by George Edmund Street, to the main body of the church. G E Street had also designed a courtyard to the south of the church, which included an arched entrance gateway, rectory, stables, school and schoolmaster's house. These are built in brick with dark blue brick stripes, while the church is brick with stone bands, dressings and spire. The church is one of Street's finest and delighted his contemporaries.

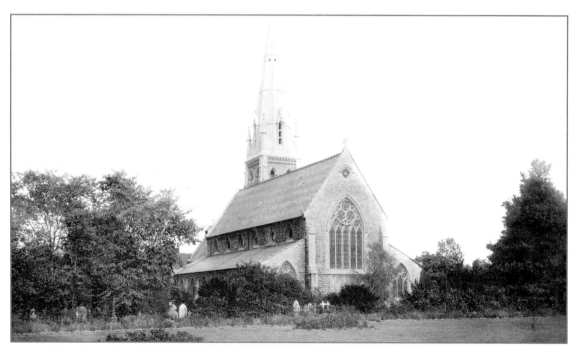

Maidenhead, St Luke's Church 1896 37916
Much more pedestrian in style is St Luke's, at the junction of St Luke's Road and Norfolk Road to the north of the town centre, built to serve the new suburb beyond what became Kidwell's Park. Typical of its era, this 1860s church is in the Decorated Gothic style built in a rock-faced stone. The field has subsequently been developed. The right-hand half is occupied by 26 Norfolk Road, and the rest by houses in Vicarage Road.

Maidenhead
St Luke's Church, from the south-west 1896 37917
Seen from Dorset Road, the tower originally had a short pyramidal tiled roof. In 1894 James Oldrid Scott, one of the George Gilbert Scott dynasty of architects, added the spire, which certainly improved its appearance. There is also a more recent flat-roofed vestry in the angle of the tower and chancel, in matching rock-cut stone. On the right is the gable of the former Maidenhead Working Men's Club, now St Luke's Hall and bereft of its barge-boards and railings.

Maidenhead Bridge and the River Thames

Maidenhead, Bridge Road 1904 52376
We now focus on the river Thames; Maidenhead's fine road bridge can be seen in the far distance. The buildings on the right have gone. On the left are the 1930s houses of Ray's Drive, occupying part of the former grounds of Ray Lodge. The grounds were progressively developed for middle class housing from the 1970s onwards. Surprisingly, Ray Lodge itself survives amid the housing.

▼ Maidenhead, Ray Park Avenue 1911 63815

Ray Park Avenue was one of the first roads laid out and has some houses of the 1870s. It is in effect the north-south spine road of the prosperous middle class estate as far north as Ray Mill Road East, the north limit of Ray Lodge's former grounds. This view has changed: both houses have been replaced by three storey blocks of flats, West Coign House on the left and Servite House on the right.

▼ Maidenhead, Turnpike 1899 43037

Until 1903, Maidenhead Bridge was a toll bridge with its neat pyramid-roofed lodges either side of the gate. Tolls had been collected since the Middle Ages on its predecessor, and the practice continued on the 1770s replacement, partly to recoup the £19,000 cost of the five-year rebuilding. In 1903, through the efforts of Joseph Taylor, the tolls were abolished and the delighted citizenry threw the gates into the river. The toll lodges were also demolished almost immediately.

▲ Maidenhead
View from Bridge 1904
52374

We are looking along Bridge Road towards Maidenhead. There is now a very busy roundabout at the junction with Ray Mead Road, which leads to Cookham. On the right is the creeper-clad Bridge House, long gone, its site now occupied by a large Texaco garage. The trees in the distance screen the remaining grounds of Ray Lodge, as yet undeveloped in 1904.

◀ **Maidenhead Thames Hotel 1893** 31755

Further north from Maidenhead Bridge, the somewhat gaunt Thames Hotel was built for Woodhouse, already an established boat builder and hirer of pleasure craft. The hotel was a great success with its genial host and principal rooms with balconies overlooking the river. In this view, the building has already been extended past the second dormer from the right. Beyond is one of Woodhouse's new boathouses and workshops.

Maidenhead, Thames Hotel 1890 23630
This view taken from near Skindles Hotel, Thames Hotel's main rival, is interesting. It shows not only Woodhouse's earlier boat workshops, replaced by 1893, but also the tree-filled grounds of Ray Lodge to the left, soon to be developed with riverside houses. The river front now has an embankment and the left side of the view is now occupied by Chandlers Quay, a block of 1998 flats and apartments.

Maidenhead, View across River 1899 43033
This is taken six years later from the same view (see above), looking due west. The bridge is visible on the left; opposite are the gardens to the river in front of Bridge House. Ray Mead Road passes between the gardens, which partly survive, and Bridge House. Sadly Bridge House is no more: a Texaco garage does not seem an equitable exchange in townscape terms. The modern Chandlers Quay flats occupy the river front to the right.

Maidenhead, Skindles Hotel 1925 77622
How the mighty are fallen! The legendary Skindles Hotel, formerly the 'premier sporting hotel on the Thames', today sits with its riverside buildings boarded up and empty, while its block east of Mill Lane is completely demolished. Formerly the Orkney Arms, it was bought in 1833 by William Skindle, who renamed it the snappier 'Skindles'. He and his son made it the most fashionable hotel to be seen at, boosting Maidenhead's late 19th-century resort status.

Maidenhead, Skindles Hotel 1906 54092
Curiously, as the Skindles Hotel expanded, it was cut in two by Mill Lane (which led to Taplow Mills). This view is from the Buckinghamshire bank, looking north from the A4 Bath Road immediately east of the bridge. The river-front buildings are on the left of the lane with the mill buildings in the distance; the 1860s block is on the right. The latter is demolished but note its then up-to-the-minute plate glass windows.

**Maidenhead
Mill House 1899**

43038
This view of the Mill
House, further north
along the
Buckinghamshire bank,
captures wonderfully
the curious formality of
late Victorian leisure
activity as the fishermen
sit stiffly in their
moored punt, solemnly
fishing. The men wear
mostly caps and jackets
while the boy on the left
sports an Eton collar.
The tent was no doubt
erected as part of
another formal leisure
activity.

▼ **Maidenhead, Mill House 1906** 54093

Here, looking towards the mill and its Victorian mill house, the view today is almost wholly screened by alders, willows and poplars. The mill has been demolished and replaced by a modern warehouse-style building, so the screening has benefits. Mill House can today only be glimpsed through trees. Note the well-pollarded willows and neat lawns of 1906 providing a better view for the couple working their punt upstream.

▼ **Maidenhead, Bridge and Riviera Hotel 1893** 31751

Passing downstream of the bridge, we see the Riviera which is still an hotel. Built as riverside apartments in the early 1880s, it was converted to an hotel in 1891 as visitor demand burgeoned. Balconies were added with glazed public rooms looking onto the river. The boathouses between it and the bridge were those of the Maidenhead Rowing Club. Rich guests at the hotel must have felt that they somewhat lowered the tone.

▲ **Maidenhead Bridge and Riviera Hotel 1899** 43031
Further along the Buckinghamshire bank we see the long side elevation of the Riviera Hotel, the name no doubt cashing in on the popularity of the French Riviera at the time. To the right is the side of Bond's boathouse, a long established boatyard with balconies to the river for viewing regattas. Sadly, at time of writing in 2001, the building is today utterly derelict and virtually beyond repair.

◀ **Maidenhead Bridge 1906** 54099
A little further south, this is the best view in the book of Sir Robert Taylor's superb seven-arch bridge, built between 1772 and 1777. Its arches are emphasised by massive, rusticated voussoir blocks, all crowned by a delicate balustrade. It is surely worth every penny of its £19,000 cost. On the right is Bond's boatyard. The Edwardian ladies are enjoying a motor trip along the river bank lane.

Maidenhead, The Thames c1960 M7037
This view shows the Riviera Hotel greatly enlarged, but with its riverside balconies entirely replaced. The Maidenhead Rowing Club boathouses are now rebuilt and smarter. The boathouse on the far left survives, and the brickwork of the hotel has been painted a cream colour.

Maidenhead, View from Bridge 1925 77615
Looking south-east from Maidenhead Bridge, Bond's boatyard with its balconies is on the left. To its right, the Maidenhead Rowing Club's superb new headquarters, completed in 1998, now stand. Balconied houses, built circa 1900, lead us to the pedestrian arch of Isambard Kingdom Brunel's remarkable railway bridge, opened in 1839 and skilfully doubled in width in the 1890s. It was built for his Great Western Railway line from Paddington to Bristol.

Maidenhead, Showing the Two Bridges 1925 77618
We look back through one of Brunel's astoundingly shallow arches to Taylor's superb road bridge of a mere sixty years earlier. Each major span of Brunel's bridge is 128 feet wide and is almost flat at the apex. Brunel proved the cynics who said it would collapse wrong: the timbering used to support the brickwork survived while the mortar set was swept away in a storm! The arches remain perfectly stable to this day.

Around Boulters Lock

Maidenhead, Boulters Lock 1906 54087
The following views focus on Boulters Lock, whose island can be seen in the distance. The Promenade along the riverbank from the bridge to Boulters Lock was completed only in Edwardian times, but was important to Maidenhead's resort status. The launch on the right is sporting the American flag: could it be the American Lady Astor of Cliveden's boat?

**Maidenhead
Boulters Lock 1906**
54083
Steamers and launches
on the right; punts, skiffs
and anything man or
woman powered on the
left. This was the
Edwardian rule and here
we see craft queuing on
a Summer weekend to
get past Boulters Lock
into Cliveden and Taplow
Reach. Note the awnings
to give shade and the
odd substantial picnic
hamper. Boats were
often moored at Glen
Island opposite, waiting
to be called through,
sometimes for hours.

▼ **Maidenhead, View from Boulters Lock 1896** 37913
This view looks downstream from the footbridge onto Ray Mill Island.
A smart houseboat is towed out by a steam launch; relatively few
boats are out. Later views illustrate the great boating craze of the
1880s which ran right up until World War I. On Ascot Sunday, 1888,
over 800 boats and 72 steam launches passed through the lock in
one day, and traffic only increased over the years.

▼ **Maidenhead, Boulters Lock Bridge 1906** 54082
The view looking towards the bridge to Ray Mill Island (or, as some
people call it, Boulters Lock Island) is the same that Edward Gregory
painted in his famous 'Boulters Lock, Sunday Afternoon' (1882-1897),
which wonderfully evokes the milling chaos of a Summer weekend.
The painting even features himself lounging in a boat near the bridge.
He lived his last few years upstream in Marlow and is buried in its
parish churchyard by the river.

▲ **Maidenhead
Boulters Lock
The Elevator 1913**
65545
Moving onto the island
itself, this was the mill rac
to Ray Mill, demolished
circa 1910. When the loc
was enlarged in 1912, the
Thames Conservancy
diverted the stream and
installed a boat elevator,
replacing an earlier
version. A series of roller
with blocks upon which
the boat sat, this looks
slightly alarming. On a
busy Summer Sunday the
elevator saved the lock
itself having to handle
over a thousand small
boats.

◄ **Maidenhead Boulters Lock 1913** 65542
Back at the lock, this view looks upstream from the bridge onto Ray Mill Island and into the newly widened lock. This increased capacity from that of the narrower 1772 original, which had been designed solely for commercial barges, not for flotillas, squadrons and armadas of pleasure craft of all shapes and sizes.

**Maidenhead
Boulters Lock and
Bridge 1913** 65544
The bridge Edward
Gregory showed in his
1880s painting
'Boulters Lock, Sunday
Afternoon' was also
replaced in 1912 with
this smart, balustraded
parapet version. On the
right is the mill house
which became the
Boulters Lock Hotel and
is now the Boulters Inn
and Restaurant. Here
we see another quieter
moment before the First
World War and
(libertarian times
indeed) ladies punting.

**Maidenhead
Boulters Lock 1925**
77624
After World War I, river cruising recovered its popularity. Here we see a mix of steam launches, punts, skiffs and rowing boats with an electric boat on the right. The island itself is now mostly a most attractive public park with a walk around its periphery and refreshment facilities, always crucial on a hot day.

Maidenhead
Boulters Lock c1955 M7054
By the 1950s, motor launches had appeared. Jerome K Jerome,
whose 'Three Men in a Boat' captured the 1880s boating scene,
wrote that oarsmen and punters loathed the steam launches and
their arrogant wakes, and went out of their way to annoy them.
This resulted in uneasy truces in the confines of the locks. Boulters
Lock is just as busy today, as is the Promenade: Maidenhead's
River Thames is still thriving.

The River Thames from Medmenham to Bray

Medmenham
The Abbey 1890 23715
The medieval arches and tower of Medmenham Abbey, on the
Berkshire bank, are fake: they are mostly embellishments to the
south wing of an Elizabethan house. Only fragments of the 13th-
century Cistercian abbey remain. From 1775-1783 it was rented
by the notorious Sir Francis Dashwood and used by the Order
of St Francis of Wycombe ('the Hell-Fire Club') who behaved like
true Georgian libertines. In 1898 the house was restored for
Robert Hudson, the soap king.

◄ **Bisham**
The Abbey 1893 31737
Today, many know Bisham Abbey as the training ground of the England football team. Indeed, it is the National Sports Centre with many new specialised buildings, sports pitches, etc. However the Abbey building does incorporate remains of Bisham Abbey. Originally a Knights Templar house, it became a priory in 1337, was promoted to abbey in 1537, only to be dissolved by Henry VIII three years later. The Hobys took over in 1540 and rebuilt it, adding the triple-turreted tower in 1560.

◀ Bisham
Abbey and Church 1890 27237

Moving further downstream towards Marlow, we reach Bisham on the Berkshire side, seen here from the towpath just beyond Marlow's Higginson Park. The tower is the chief glory of the chalkstone church, dating from about 1170. The rest of the church has been heavily restored, if not rebuilt, apart from the Tudor Hoby Chapel which contains some excellent monuments. To the right looms Bisham Abbey, while ladies row themselves gently upstream on a gentle Summer's day.

▼ Marlow
Complete Angler Hotel 1890
23679

The popular Complete Angler Hotel lies on the Berkshire bank and looks out across the Thames to Marlow. Originally, the road crossed a bridge to its left, but since 1832 the present superb suspension bridge has taken the road to the right, allowing the hotel to steadily expand towards the western route. Here we look past the hotel and the weir towards Lock Island from the 1832 bridge, before the hotel's 20th-century expansion.

◀ Marlow
The Lock 1890 23681

This view looks west towards the Parish church. The pound lock replaced the hazardous flash locks in the middle of the weir in 1773. However this exacerbated the flooding of the churchyard and the medieval parish church partially collapsed. In 1832 it was replaced and here we see the knobbly spire of that date. It was later replaced by the present elegant one by John Oldrid Scott, who also designed the spire of St Luke's in Maidenhead.

Marlow, Mills 1890 27234

Just beyond the lock exit were the corn (later thimble and oil) mills. Even later converted to paper mills, they were rebuilt after a fire in 1825 and continued in use until 1935. They were finally demolished in 1965 and the site is now occupied by three-storey houses with weatherboarded elevations and a vaguely watermill/warehouse feel. This view is from Lock island, which since about 1890 has been filled with houses and bungalows of distinctly variable quality.

Cookham Dean, Winter Hill 1925 77595

Winter Hill is a noted beauty spot on the Berkshire side with views along the Thames. The hill rises about 180 feet above the river and gives superb views of the valley below. Much of the best part is now owned by the National Trust, who also own a fair amount of Cookham Dean's open space. Here we see a car toiling up the hill from the Cookham direction. Nowadays the slopes are more overgrown.

Cookham Dean, The Village 1901 47119
This view shows Cookham Dean and captures the deeply rural nature of the area before this post-1900 development changed it forever. Cookham Dean comprises various clusters of settlement - Dean Bottom, Starling's Green, Winter Hill and the Mount - but has no real centre. It had a reputation for lawlessness amid the thatched cottages, some of which can be seen in this view, but it is overwhelmingly respectable and middle class nowadays.

Bourne End, Marina and Boatyard 1899 43963
East of Marlow, where the river bends south, Townsend's and Shaw's boatyards and their wharves were a focus of boating activity in the heyday of the late Victorian and Edwardian boating boom. The renowned Bourne End Regatta was based here, established in 1897, with the club house to the right of Shaw's boat works. Here we see the 1899 Regatta in a lull between races, with a picnic taking place on board the moored steam launch 'Cynisca'.

◄ **Cookham**
The River 1901 47115
The celebrated village of Cookham, a mile or so south of Bourne End, is seen here from the boatyard on the Buckinghamshire bank, although curiously until 1992 a strip of about 30 feet along this side was within Berkshire. The bridge dates from 1867. The church's west tower is 15th-century. This churchyard was the setting for Sir Stanley Spencer's famous painting of the Resurrection, and the artist is buried here.

Bourne End
Furlong Road c1955 B160026

Beyond the boatyards, Bourne End grew up as a somewhat amorphous settlement around the railway station on the Maidenhead to High Wycombe line, which opened in 1854. In 1873 a branch line opened along the north bank of the Thames to Marlow, hauled by the famous 'Marlow Donkey' steam engine. The Wycombe to Bourne End section closed years ago, but Bourne End continued to expand. Here the Edwardian shopping parades along Furlong Road give a flavour.

Cookham
Bell and Dragon 1899

43030

Away from the river in Cookham village, we look east along the High Street to the Sutton Road and Ferry Lane junction. The river is off to the left. Beyond the creeper-clad building on the right is the old Methodist chapel of 1846, now the Stanley Spencer Gallery.

Cookham
High Street 1914 67016

Further west along the High Street, the road is dominated by the Kings Arms Hotel, which seems curiously out of scale with its surroundings. To the right are hedges and dwarf walls in front of the 1870s pair of semi-detached houses. Sir Stanley Spencer was born in the right-hand house, Fernley, in 1891, and lived there for much of his somewhat eccentric life.

**Cookham
High Street 1908** 61017
Even further west in the
High Street, we see a
motorist climbing in or
out of his car in an
otherwise traffic-less
street, very much unlike
the present day. The
Royal Exchange, from
where the Edwardian
visitor could telephone, is
now a tandoori restaurant
but remains creeper-clad.
The properties beyond
are not, but their
flintwork elevations are
now fully exposed. Note
the row of timber-framed
17th-century cottages on
the right.

▼ Cookham, The Moor 1901 47114

A causeway had to be built across Cookham Moor as the area is so prone to flooding. Indeed, one of the causeway bridges was swept away by flooding in 1774. One of the two places where the Thames regularly overflows is Cookham Moor, and locals there need no reminder of the winter floods of 2000-2001.

▼ Cookham, The Pound 1914 67013

West of Cookham Moor there were a few farmhouses and cottages, but the arrival of the Maidenhead to Wycombe Railway line and station in 1854 led to great expansion. The Pound is the name given to an enclosure for stray animals, now gone. This view looks across the Moor, seen beyond the gate pier and the 17th-century timber-framed Old Farmhouse. All the buildings survive, with the White Hart now Spencers, a popular pub-restaurant. There is a mini-roundabout at the Terry's Lane junction.

▲ Cookham, Station Hill 1914 67009

Further up Station Road, we are now at the approach to Cookham Station at the top of Station Hill. The road leads downhill to the Pound and the Moor, beyond the distant Old Anchor Inn (currently closed in 2001). The two late Victorian buildings on the left remain: St Anne's House on the left is a dentist's surgery and Shergolds, the fruiterers and florist, is now Village Hardware. Partly obscured by conifers is Seaton Cottage, dated 1884.

Cookham
Odney Common 1925
77588
Back at the river, the Thames approaches the Cliveden cliffs tentatively, breaking up into numerous channels and islands. The meanders were by-passed by the main river via the Lock Cut of 1830; Cookham has the benefit of Odney Common, an island along the north side of one of the channels. This view south is little changed, apart from a footbridge in the middle distance. People still picnic and walk here.

◀ **Cliveden**
Cliveden House 1893 31758
Cliveden benefits from a
breathtaking river view from its
terraces. Built on a 1660s
terrace, today's Cliveden is a
Victorian mansion by Sir Charles
Barry, one of the architects of the
Houses of Parliament. Completed
in 1851 for the Duke of
Sutherland, the magnificent
house is now a country house
hotel. Owned by the National
Trust, its grounds are open most
of the year. The house is more
well-known for its past
associations with the Astors and
Christine Keeler.

◀ **Cliveden**
Cliveden Woods 1925 77613
Between Cookham and Boulters Lock, the River Thames cuts close to the Buckinghamshire bank to form beautiful tree-clad river-cliffs rising 150 feet to the chalk plateau above. This is widely regarded as one of the most beautiful stretches of the Thames. In this view a punt takes the wash of a steam launch. The mansion of Cliveden can be seen above the trees. The Berkshire bank is now tree-lined, so this view can only be intermittently glimpsed.

▼ **Cliveden**
Ferry and Cottage 1906 54103
From the Berkshire bank we see Ferry Cottage, built in 1861 for the Duke of Sutherland to designs by George Devey. Nestling above is the dome of the 1735 Octagon Temple by Giacomo Leoni. My Lady Ferry was originally provided to carry barge-towing horses to the Berkshire side, as the Cliveden estate by the river is impassable. Now long defunct, it later became more of a ferry for visitors to Cliveden walking out from Maidenhead.

◀ **Cliveden**
The Springs 1890 23648
Looking directly across the river from the Berkshire side, this view gives a good idea of the dramatic beauty that so appealed during the 19th century. Below the towering trees is The Springs, now Spring Cottage, of 1857. Also by George Devey, it incorporates the Gothick spring house of 1813 by Peter Nicholson. After this view was taken, Ralph Waldo Storey added balustrades and steps to the river front in the mid-1890s for Lord Astor.

Taplow, The Village 1906 54109
Taplow village is set at the end of the chalk ridge south of Cliveden, where it drops down towards the Bath Road. Its principal house, Taplow Court, now a Tudor-Gothic 1840s style mansion, commands a wonderful view over the Thames valley, as does Cliveden. In this view, Berry Hill begins its steep descent off the chalk plateau. The thatched cottage was replaced by a larger Arts and Crafts version by the Taplow Estate around 1900.

Burnham, High Street c1955 B250011
Burnham desperately struggles to keep its identity separate from the sprawl of Slough, but the historic core is surrounded by suburban housing and its main street has seen injudicious change since 1955. Much survives, but in this view from the junction with Gore Road, the Slough and District Co-op on the left and the buildings beyond have all gone, although those on the right remain. W H Cleare is now a restaurant rather than a contractors and coal factors.

Burnham, Burnham Beeches 1929 81697
Burnham Beeches are well-known, having been saved for the nation by the Corporation of London in 1880, following pressure from a Victorian naturalist named Heath. The Corporation bought about 80 hectares for the enjoyment of all, but particularly (as with Epping Forest and Hampstead Heath) as a 'green lung' for Londoners. Neglected since coal finally supplanted wood as a fuel for Londoners around 1800, these ancient pollarded beeches lie north-east of Burnham on sandy soils, now somewhat constricted by rhododendrons.

Holyport, Main Road 1909 61983
Holyport, two miles south of Maidenhead was originally 'Horipod' or dirty market town. By the 18th century it had civilised itself to 'Hollyport' and by the early 19th century had assumed an odour of sanctity with 'Holyport'. The cottage Fiddlers Folly on the left is now largely rebuilt. All else survives except the shop-in-a-shed. This is the frantically busy A330 and the wall on the right, to Holyport Lodge, has been moved back for road widening.

◀ **Holyport, Stud Green 1909** 61990
Farther down the A330 is Stud Green, a hamlet of Holyport. Its character is now largely suburban, following much rebuilding. This view looks west. The Bricklayers Arms is now a house, Old Brick House, its brickwork painted. The farm building on the left in yellow London stock brick has been converted into a house, Walnut Barn. The farmhouse, (out of shot to the left), Walnut Cottage, and some frontage walling also survives.

Holyport, The Green
1909 61984

The wide green east of the busy A330 is still attractive, although the pond has long been filled in. A sundial to commemorate the millennium has been added. The cottages from the previous view (see 61983 page 81) are on the left. Holyport Lodge, the white house, is now substantially enlarged as a private nursing home. The late 19th-century timber-framed pair on the right, Warden House and Glenside, also remain, as does the 16th-century timber-framed cottage, Little Tudor, at the far left.

Waltham St Lawrence
The Street c1955 W377013

Waltham St Lawrence and White Waltham lie some four to five miles south-west of Maidenhead. They take their name from Waltham Abbey in Essex, the royal manor of which they were a part. Well into the 19th century, Waltham St Lawrence was known as St Laurence Waltham. Here we look north along The Street toward the parish church. The post office and thatched barn are now houses.

Waltham St Lawrence
Village c1955 W377001

From within the lychgate of the medieval parish church, we look at Waltham St Lawrence's finest building: the 14th century Bell Inn. This 'Wealden' house with its jettied crosswings and central hall under a single roof was given to the parish by Ralph Newbery in 1608. He was a local boy made good as a citizen of London and a member of the Stationers Company. To the left is the 15th-century Bell Cottage.

Bray, Jesus Hospital 1890
23624
A little further south, is Jesus Hospital, a fine quadrangle of 28 single-storey almshouses with a taller entrance bay. A stern notice in the entrance archway states that 'Vagrants, Hawkers and Dogs Are Not Admitted'. It was founded in 1627 by William Goddard, a local man made good as citizen of London and member of the Fishmongers Company. He is commemorated with a statue and his monument is in the church.

Bray, The Village 1911 63821
A former royal manor, Bray is well known for the song 'The Vicar of Bray', celebrating the vicar who changed sides several times during the Civil War and after to keep his living. The tranquillity of this delightful village is traffic-blighted, like many in the area. Here we look along the High Street towards the junction with Church Lane. At the end is the Hind's Head Hotel. The Ringers on the right is now the Fat Duck Restaurant. The timber-framed cottages have long gone.

Bray, On the Thames 1929
81695
From the High Street, Ferry Lane leads down to the river and the former ferry point. We are looking back up the lane with the river behind us. On the right is part of the George Hotel, as it was then. The view is little changed apart from the outbuilding on the right with the two dormer windows which is now a house, Tansy Cottage.

Bray, Landing Place 1890
23621
Here we are standing on the slipway where Ferry Lane disappears into the River Thames. The straw-hatted boy peers round the fence of the George Hotel from its riverside garden; another boy fishes. The George is now the renowned Waterside Inn with a thoroughly developed river terrace that includes an oriental-style gazebo. In the distance is part of the Fishery Estate along Bray Reach, started in the 1890s by a rich widow named Annie Smith.

Bray, Monkey Island 1890 23611

About a mile downstream from Bray is the curiously named Monkey Island. It gets its name from the Duke of Marlborough's fishing lodge, built around 1744, in which a room was painted by noted monkey artist Clermont as a 'singerie', with scenes of monkeys fishing, shooting and following outdoor sports. The Temple, seen here, had an open ground floor and first floor rooms. Now attached to a house, the whole complex is part of the successful Monkey Island Hotel.

Dorney, The Reach 1951 D87007

Our last view shows Dorney Reach with the Berkshire bank on the left. This tranquil stretch of towing path, now part of the splendid Thames Path long distance footpath, has had its tranquillity rudely shattered. Now, in the middle distance an elegant duck egg blue-painted steel bridge carries the ceaseless roar of the M4 motorway across the River Thames, in effect the latest Maidenhead by-pass.

Index

Frith Book Co Titles

www.francisfrith.co.uk

The Frith Book Company publishes over 100 new titles each year. A selection of those currently available are listed below. For latest catalogue please contact Frith Book Co.

Town Books 96 pages, approx 100 photos. County and Themed Books 128 pages, approx 150 photos (unless specified). All titles hardback laminated case and jacket except those indicated pb (paperback)

Title	ISBN	Price	Title	ISBN	Price
Amersham, Chesham & Rickmansworth (pb)			Derby (pb)	1-85937-367-4	£9.99
	1-85937-340-2	£9.99	Derbyshire (pb)	1-85937-196-5	£9.99
Ancient Monuments & Stone Circles	1-85937-143-4	£17.99	Devon (pb)	1-85937-297-x	£9.99
Aylesbury (pb)	1-85937-227-9	£9.99	Dorset (pb)	1-85937-269-4	£9.99
Bakewell	1-85937-113-2	£12.99	Dorset Churches	1-85937-172-8	£17.99
Barnstaple (pb)	1-85937-300-3	£9.99	Dorset Coast (pb)	1-85937-299-6	£9.99
Bath (pb)	1-85937-419-0	£9.99	Dorset Living Memories	1-85937-210-4	£14.99
Bedford (pb)	1-85937-205-8	£9.99	Down the Severn	1-85937-118-3	£14.99
Berkshire (pb)	1-85937-191-4	£9.99	Down the Thames (pb)	1-85937-278-3	£9.99
Berkshire Churches	1-85937-170-1	£17.99	Down the Trent	1-85937-311-9	£14.99
Blackpool (pb)	1-85937-382-8	£9.99	Dublin (pb)	1-85937-231-7	£9.99
Bognor Regis (pb)	1-85937-431-x	£9.99	East Anglia (pb)	1-85937-265-1	£9.99
Bournemouth	1-85937-067-5	£12.99	East London	1-85937-080-2	£14.99
Bradford (pb)	1-85937-204-x	£9.99	East Sussex	1-85937-130-2	£14.99
Brighton & Hove(pb)	1-85937-192-2	£8.99	Eastbourne	1-85937-061-6	£12.99
Bristol (pb)	1-85937-264-3	£9.99	Edinburgh (pb)	1-85937-193-0	£8.99
British Life A Century Ago (pb)	1-85937-213-9	£9.99	England in the 1880s	1-85937-331-3	£17.99
Buckinghamshire (pb)	1-85937-200-7	£9.99	English Castles (pb)	1-85937-434-4	£9.99
Camberley (pb)	1-85937-222-8	£9.99	English Country Houses	1-85937-161-2	£17.99
Cambridge (pb)	1-85937-422-0	£9.99	Essex (pb)	1-85937-270-8	£9.99
Cambridgeshire (pb)	1-85937-420-4	£9.99	Exeter	1-85937-126-4	£12.99
Canals & Waterways (pb)	1-85937-291-0	£9.99	Exmoor	1-85937-132-9	£14.99
Canterbury Cathedral (pb)	1-85937-179-5	£9.99	Falmouth	1-85937-066-7	£12.99
Cardiff (pb)	1-85937-093-4	£9.99	Folkestone (pb)	1-85937-124-8	£9.99
Carmarthenshire	1-85937-216-3	£14.99	Glasgow (pb)	1-85937-190-6	£9.99
Chelmsford (pb)	1-85937-310-0	£9.99	Gloucestershire	1-85937-102-7	£14.99
Cheltenham (pb)	1-85937-095-0	£9.99	Great Yarmouth (pb)	1-85937-426-3	£9.99
Cheshire (pb)	1-85937-271-6	£9.99	Greater Manchester (pb)	1-85937-266-x	£9.99
Chester	1-85937-090-x	£12.99	Guildford (pb)	1-85937-410-7	£9.99
Chesterfield	1-85937-378-x	£9.99	Hampshire (pb)	1-85937-279-1	£9.99
Chichester (pb)	1-85937-228-7	£9.99	Hampshire Churches (pb)	1-85937-207-4	£9.99
Colchester (pb)	1-85937-188-4	£8.99	Harrogate	1-85937-423-9	£9.99
Cornish Coast	1-85937-163-9	£14.99	Hastings & Bexhill (pb)	1-85937-131-0	£9.99
Cornwall (pb)	1-85937-229-5	£9.99	Heart of Lancashire (pb)	1-85937-197-3	£9.99
Cornwall Living Memories	1-85937-248-1	£14.99	Helston (pb)	1-85937-214-7	£9.99
Cotswolds (pb)	1-85937-230-9	£9.99	Hereford (pb)	1-85937-175-2	£9.99
Cotswolds Living Memories	1-85937-255-4	£14.99	Herefordshire	1-85937-174-4	£14.99
County Durham	1-85937-123-x	£14.99	Hertfordshire (pb)	1-85937-247-3	£9.99
Croydon Living Memories	1-85937-162-0	£9.99	Horsham (pb)	1-85937-432-8	£9.99
Cumbria	1-85937-101-9	£14.99	Humberside	1-85937-215-5	£14.99
Dartmoor	1-85937-145-0	£14.99	Hythe, Romney Marsh & Ashford	1-85937-256-2	£9.99

Available from your local bookshop or from the publisher

Frith Book Co Titles (continued)

Title	ISBN	Price	Title	ISBN	Price
Ipswich (pb)	1-85937-424-7	£9.99	St Ives (pb)	1-85937415-8	£9.99
Ireland (pb)	1-85937-181-7	£9.99	Scotland (pb)	1-85937-182-5	£9.99
Isle of Man (pb)	1-85937-268-6	£9.99	Scottish Castles (pb)	1-85937-323-2	£9.99
Isles of Scilly	1-85937-136-1	£14.99	Sevenoaks & Tunbridge	1-85937-057-8	£12.99
Isle of Wight (pb)	1-85937-429-8	£9.99	Sheffield, South Yorks (pb)	1-85937-267-8	£9.99
Isle of Wight Living Memories	1-85937-304-6	£14.99	Shrewsbury (pb)	1-85937-325-9	£9.99
Kent (pb)	1-85937-189-2	£9.99	Shropshire (pb)	1-85937-326-7	£9.99
Kent Living Memories	1-85937-125-6	£14.99	Somerset	1-85937-153-1	£14.99
Lake District (pb)	1-85937-275-9	£9.99	South Devon Coast	1-85937-107-8	£14.99
Lancaster, Morecambe & Heysham (pb)	1-85937-233-3	£9.99	South Devon Living Memories	1-85937-168-x	£14.99
Leeds (pb)	1-85937-202-3	£9.99	South Hams	1-85937-220-1	£14.99
Leicester	1-85937-073-x	£12.99	Southampton (pb)	1-85937-427-1	£9.99
Leicestershire (pb)	1-85937-185-x	£9.99	Southport (pb)	1-85937-425-5	£9.99
Lincolnshire (pb)	1-85937-433-6	£9.99	Staffordshire	1-85937-047-0	£12.99
Liverpool & Merseyside (pb)	1-85937-234-1	£9.99	Stratford upon Avon	1-85937-098-5	£12.99
London (pb)	1-85937-183-3	£9.99	Suffolk (pb)	1-85937-221-x	£9.99
Ludlow (pb)	1-85937-176-0	£9.99	Suffolk Coast	1-85937-259-7	£14.99
Luton (pb)	1-85937-235-x	£9.99	Surrey (pb)	1-85937-240-6	£9.99
Maidstone	1-85937-056-x	£14.99	Sussex (pb)	1-85937-184-1	£9.99
Manchester (pb)	1-85937-198-1	£9.99	Swansea (pb)	1-85937-167-1	£9.99
Middlesex	1-85937-158-2	£14.99	Tees Valley & Cleveland	1-85937-211-2	£14.99
New Forest	1-85937-128-0	£14.99	Thanet (pb)	1-85937-116-7	£9.99
Newark (pb)	1-85937-366-6	£9.99	Tiverton (pb)	1-85937-178-7	£9.99
Newport, Wales (pb)	1-85937-258-9	£9.99	Torbay	1-85937-063-2	£12.99
Newquay (pb)	1-85937-421-2	£9.99	Truro	1-85937-147-7	£12.99
Norfolk (pb)	1-85937-195-7	£9.99	Victorian and Edwardian Cornwall	1-85937-252-x	£14.99
Norfolk Living Memories	1-85937-217-1	£14.99	Victorian & Edwardian Devon	1-85937-253-8	£14.99
Northamptonshire	1-85937-150-7	£14.99	Victorian & Edwardian Kent	1-85937-149-3	£14.99
Northumberland Tyne & Wear (pb)	1-85937-281-3	£9.99	Vic & Ed Maritime Album	1-85937-144-2	£17.99
North Devon Coast	1-85937-146-9	£14.99	Victorian and Edwardian Sussex	1-85937-157-4	£14.99
North Devon Living Memories	1-85937-261-9	£14.99	Victorian & Edwardian Yorkshire	1-85937-154-x	£14.99
North London	1-85937-206-6	£14.99	Victorian Seaside	1-85937-159-0	£17.99
North Wales (pb)	1-85937-298-8	£9.99	Villages of Devon (pb)	1-85937-293-7	£9.99
North Yorkshire (pb)	1-85937-236-8	£9.99	Villages of Kent (pb)	1-85937-294-5	£9.99
Norwich (pb)	1-85937-194-9	£8.99	Villages of Sussex (pb)	1-85937-295-3	£9.99
Nottingham (pb)	1-85937-324-0	£9.99	Warwickshire (pb)	1-85937-203-1	£9.99
Nottinghamshire (pb)	1-85937-187-6	£9.99	Welsh Castles (pb)	1-85937-322-4	£9.99
Oxford (pb)	1-85937-411-5	£9.99	West Midlands (pb)	1-85937-289-9	£9.99
Oxfordshire (pb)	1-85937-430-1	£9.99	West Sussex	1-85937-148-5	£14.99
Peak District (pb)	1-85937-280-5	£9.99	West Yorkshire (pb)	1-85937-201-5	£9.99
Penzance	1-85937-069-1	£12.99	Weymouth (pb)	1-85937-209-0	£9.99
Peterborough (pb)	1-85937-219-8	£9.99	Wiltshire (pb)	1-85937-277-5	£9.99
Piers	1-85937-237-6	£17.99	Wiltshire Churches (pb)	1-85937-171-x	£9.99
Plymouth	1-85937-119-1	£12.99	Wiltshire Living Memories	1-85937-245-7	£14.99
Poole & Sandbanks (pb)	1-85937-251-1	£9.99	Winchester (pb)	1-85937-428-x	£9.99
Preston (pb)	1-85937-212-0	£9.99	Windmills & Watermills	1-85937-242-2	£17.99
Reading (pb)	1-85937-238-4	£9.99	Worcester (pb)	1-85937-165-5	£9.99
Romford (pb)	1-85937-319-4	£9.99	Worcestershire	1-85937-152-3	£14.99
Salisbury (pb)	1-85937-239-2	£9.99	York (pb)	1-85937-199-x	£9.99
Scarborough (pb)	1-85937-379-8	£9.99	Yorkshire (pb)	1-85937-186-8	£9.99
St Albans (pb)	1-85937-341-0	£9.99	Yorkshire Living Memories	1-85937-166-3	£14.99

See Frith books on the internet www.francisfrith.co.uk

FRITH PRODUCTS & SERVICES

Francis Frith would doubtless be pleased to know that the pioneering publishing venture he started in 1860 still continues today. A hundred and forty years later, The Francis Frith Collection continues in the same innovative tradition and is now one of the foremost publishers of vintage photographs in the world. Some of the current activities include:

Interior Decoration

Today Frith's photographs can be seen framed and as giant wall murals in thousands of pubs, restaurants, hotels, banks, retail stores and other public buildings throughout the country. In every case they enhance the unique local atmosphere of the places they depict and provide reminders of gentler days in an increasingly busy and frenetic world.

Product Promotions

Frith products are used by many major companies to promote the sales of their own products or to reinforce their own history and heritage. Frith promotions have been used by Hovis bread, Courage beers, Scots Porage Oats, Colman's mustard, Cadbury's foods, Mellow Birds coffee, Dunhill pipe tobacco, Guinness, and Bulmer's Cider.

Genealogy and Family History

As the interest in family history and roots grows world-wide, more and more people are turning to Frith's photographs of Great Britain for images of the towns, villages and streets where their ancestors lived; and, of course, photographs of the churches and chapels where their ancestors were christened, married and buried are an essential part of every genealogy tree and family album.

Frith Products

All Frith photographs are available Framed or just as Mounted Prints and Posters (size 23 x 16 inches). These may be ordered from the address below. From time to time other products - Address Books, Calendars, Table Mats, etc - are available.

The Internet

Already twenty thousand Frith photographs can be viewed and purchased on the internet through the Frith websites and a myriad of partner sites.

For more detailed information on Frith companies and products, look at these sites:

www.francisfrith.co.uk
www.francisfrith.com
(for North American visitors)

See the complete list of Frith Books at:

www.francisfrith.co.uk

This web site is regularly updated with the latest list of publications from the Frith Book Company. If you wish to buy books relating to another part of the country that your local bookshop does not stock, you may purchase on-line.

For further information, trade, or author enquiries please contact us at the address below:
The Francis Frith Collection, Frith's Barn, Teffont, Salisbury, Wiltshire, England SP3 5QP.
Tel: +44 (0)1722 716 376 Fax: +44 (0)1722 716 881 Email: sales@francisfrith.co.uk

See Frith books on the internet www.francisfrith.co.uk

TO RECEIVE YOUR FREE MOUNTED PRINT

Mounted Print
Overall size 14 x 11 inches

Cut out this Voucher and return it with your remittance for £1.95 to cover postage and handling, to UK addresses. For overseas addresses please include £4.00 post and handling. Choose any photograph included in this book. Your SEPIA print will be A4 in size, and mounted in a cream mount with burgundy rule line, overall size 14 x 11 inches.

Order additional Mounted Prints at HALF PRICE (only £7.49 each*)

If there are further pictures you would like to order, possibly as gifts for friends and family, purchase them at half price (no additional postage and handling required).

Have your Mounted Prints framed*

For an additional £14.95 per print you can have your chosen Mounted Print framed in an elegant polished wood and gilt moulding, overall size 16 x 13 inches (no additional postage and handling required).

---

* IMPORTANT!
These special prices are only available if ordered using the original voucher on this page (no copies permitted) and at the same time as your free Mounted Print, for delivery to the same address

---

Frith Collectors' Guild

From time to time we publish a magazine of news and stories about Frith photographs and further special offers of Frith products. If you would like 12 months FREE membership, please return this form.

Send completed forms to:
The Francis Frith Collection, Frith's Barn, Teffont, Salisbury, Wiltshire SP3 5QP

Voucher for FREE and Reduced Price Frith Prints

Picture no.	Page number	Qty	Mounted @ £7.49	Framed + £14.95	Total Cost
		1	**Free of charge***	£	£
			£7.49	£	£
			£7.49	£	£
			£7.49	£	£
			£7.49	£	£
			£7.49	£	£

Please allow 28 days for delivery	*** Post & handling**	£1.95
Book Title	**Total Order Cost**	£

Please do not photocopy this voucher. Only the original is valid, so please cut it out and return it to us.

I enclose a cheque / postal order for £ . . . . made payable to 'The Francis Frith Collection' OR please debit my Mastercard / Visa / Switch / Amex card *(credit cards please on all overseas orders)*

Number . . . .

Issue No (Switch only) . . . . .Valid from (Amex/Switch) . . . .

Expires . . . . Signature . . . .

Name Mr/Mrs/Ms . . . .

Address . . . .

. . . .

. . . . Postcode . . . .

Daytime Tel No . . . .   Valid to 31/12/02

The Francis Frith Collectors' Guild

Please enrol me as a member for 12 months free of charge.

Name Mr/Mrs/Ms . . . .

Address . . . .

. . . .

. . . . Postcode . . . .

Would you like to find out more about Francis Frith?

We have recently recruited some entertaining speakers who are happy to visit local groups, clubs and societies to give an illustrated talk documenting Frith's travels and photographs. If you are a member of such a group and are interested in hosting a presentation, we would love to hear from you.

Our speakers bring with them a small selection of our local town and county books, together with sample prints. They are happy to take orders. A small proportion of the order value is donated to the group who have hosted the presentation. The talks are therefore an excellent way of fundraising for small groups and societies.

Can you help us with information about any of the Frith photographs in this book?

We are gradually compiling an historical record for each of the photographs in the Frith archive. It is always fascinating to find out the names of the people shown in the pictures, as well as insights into the shops, buildings and other features depicted.

If you recognize anyone in the photographs in this book, or if you have information not already included in the author's caption, do let us know. We would love to hear from you, and will try to publish it in future books or articles.

Our production team

Frith books are produced by a small dedicated team at offices in the converted Grade II listed 18th-century barn at Teffont near Salisbury, illustrated above. Most have worked with the Frith Collection for many years. All have in common one quality: they have a passion for the Frith Collection. The team is constantly expanding, but currently includes:

Jason Buck, John Buck, Douglas Burns, Heather Crisp, Isobel Hall, Rob Hames, Hazel Heaton, Peter Horne, James Kinnear, Tina Leary, Hannah Marsh, Eliza Sackett, Terence Sackett, Sandra Sanger, Shelley Tolcher, Susanna Walker, Clive Wathen and Jenny Wathen.